A Bean's Life

Angela Royston

Crabtree Publishing Company

www.crabtreebooks.com

Author: Angela Royston
Editors: Kathy Middleton
Crystal Sikkens
Project coordinator: Kathy Middleton
Production coordinator: Ken Wright
Prepress technicians: Ken Wright
Margaret Amy Salter

Picture Credits:
Dreamstime: Darko Plohl: pages 14–15
Photolibrary: Jeronimo Alba: page 18; Rex Butcher:
page 16; Howard Rice: page 12
Shutterstock: cover; Arteretum: page 11; Artography:
page 4; Bonchan: page 20; Nito: pages 1, 15; Optimarc:
page 19; Orientaly: page 6; Orla: page 9; Piotrwrk:
page 13; SeDmi: page 15; Sevenke: pages 3, 5; Alex
Staroseltsev: page 17; Superdumb: page 21; Bogdan
Wankowicz: pages 7, 8, 10

Every effort has been made to trace copyright holders and to obtain their
permission for use of copyright material. The authors and publishers
would be pleased to rectify any error or omission in future editions.
All the Internet addresses given in this book were correct at the time of
going to press. The author and publishers regret any inconvenience
caused if addresses have changed or sites have ceased to exist, but can
accept no responsibility for any such changes.

Library and Archives Canada Cataloguing in Publication

Royston, Angela
A bean's life / Angela Royston.

(Crabtree connections)
Includes index.
ISBN 978-0-7787-7840-0 (bound).--ISBN 978-0-7787-7862-2 (pbk.)

1. Beans--Juvenile literature. 2. Beans--Life cycles--Juvenile
literature. I. Title. II. Series: Crabtree connections

SB327.R69 2011   j635'.65   C2011-900595-6

Library of Congress Cataloging-in-Publication Data

Royston, Angela, 1945-
A bean's life / Angela Royston.
p. cm. -- (Crabtree connections)
Includes index.
ISBN 978-0-7787-7862-2 (pbk. : alk. paper) -- ISBN 978-0-7787-7840-0
(reinforced library binding : alk. paper)
1. Beans--Juvenile literature. 2. Beans--Life cycles--Juvenile
literature. 3. Growth (Plants)--Juvenile literature. I. Title.
SB327.R69 2011
633.3--dc22
                                                        2011001327

Crabtree Publishing Company

www.crabtreebooks.com   1-800-387-7650

Printed in the U.S.A./072011/WO20110114

Published in Canada
Crabtree Publishing
616 Welland Ave.
St. Catharines, Ontario
L2M 5V6

Published in the United States
Crabtree Publishing
PMB 59051
350 Fifth Avenue, 59th Floor
New York, New York 10118

Contents

What are Beans?

Beans come from plants. Many different types of beans are grown around the world.

Why are beans grown?

People grow beans because they are good to eat and can taste delicious when they are cooked. They also contain **vitamins** that keep your body healthy.

Baked beans

Baked beans are made from a type of bean called the navy bean.

Fava beans have a thick, green skin.

Colors and shapes

Different types of beans look different. Many beans are red, some are round, while other beans look like tiny eggs.

Planting Beans

Beans are **seeds** as well as food, so when a bean is planted in the soil, it grows into a plant. The plant then makes more beans.

Where do beans grow?

Fava beans grow well in cool countries. They are planted at the end of winter and can stand very cold weather. Beans are planted in long rows in the soil.

Tough stuff

Fava bean plants can grow even when the soil is covered with snow.

A tractor plants the beans and covers them with soil.

Below the soil

Inside the bean is a tiny plant. As the bean lies in the soil, the tiny plant begins to grow.

Growing in the Soil

The bean is a **store** of food that the tiny plant uses to grow bigger and bigger. After a while, the tiny plant is too big to stay inside the bean, and it bursts out of the bean's skin.

What happens next?

A **root** pushes through the skin and grows down into the soil. A green **shoot** pokes through the top of the bean and grows upward through the soil.

shoot

To the Sun

Fava bean shoots grow upward toward the sunlight at the soil's surface.

Roots and a shoot grow into the soil.

root

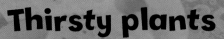

Thirsty plants

A plant needs water to grow. Its roots are covered with thin hairs that take in water from the soil.

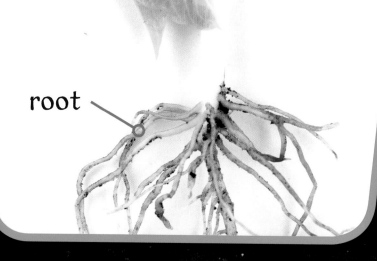

root

Breaking Through

After a few weeks, the shoot is so long that it pushes through the top of the soil. Two small leaves open up at the end of the **stem**.

stem

Why do leaves grow?

As the stem grows taller, more leaves grow. The plant has finished the food stored in the bean, so the leaves make food for the plant instead.

skin

Empty skin

The empty bean skin falls into the soil and **rots** away.

The bean plant breaks through the surface of the soil.

tube

Making food

Leaves make sugary juice from water, sunlight, and air. The juice travels along tiny tubes to the rest of the plant.

Flowers

The plant grows taller and taller and, after a few weeks, **buds** grow on the stem. They open up into small flowers.

Bees like flowers!

Bees crawl into the flowers. Inside each flower is yellow **pollen** dust, which sticks to the bees' legs and is then carried to other flowers.

A lot of flowers grow close together on the stems.

bud

Hairy bees

Bees have very hairy legs! Pollen sticks to the hairs when bees land on flowers.

pollen

Honeybee

Flowers contain a sweet juice called **nectar**. Bees make honey from nectar and store it inside their nests.

Green Pods

After the flowers have died and the petals have fallen off, a thin green **pod** grows beneath the dying flower. The pod contains tiny beans.

Why did the beans grow?

Each tiny bean grew after it joined with a grain of pollen from another flower. The beans grow bigger and the pods grow longer.

The pods grow where the flowers used to be.

How many beans?

Most fava bean pods contain between three and eight fava beans.

Safe inside

The pod is tough on the outside and fluffy on the inside to protect the growing beans.

pod

Attack!

Bean beetles and other **insects** eat the leaves of the plant. Hundreds of beetles can feed on just one plant.

Aphids harm beans

Aphids also feed on bean plants. They suck juice called **sap** from inside the plant.

Fight back

Some farmers use **chemicals** to kill the insects that attack their fava bean plants.

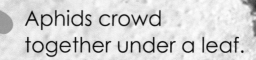
Aphids crowd together under a leaf.

Farmers' friends

Farmers like ladybugs because they love to eat the aphids.

aphid

Time to Pick

It is three or four months since the seeds were planted, and the pods are now long and fat. They are ready to be picked.

How are the beans picked?

Farmers use special machines to pick the pods. The machine pulls up the plants from the soil and shakes the beans off the plants.

The machines pick the beans in rows.

Into the soil

The plants are put back into the soil once the beans have been picked.

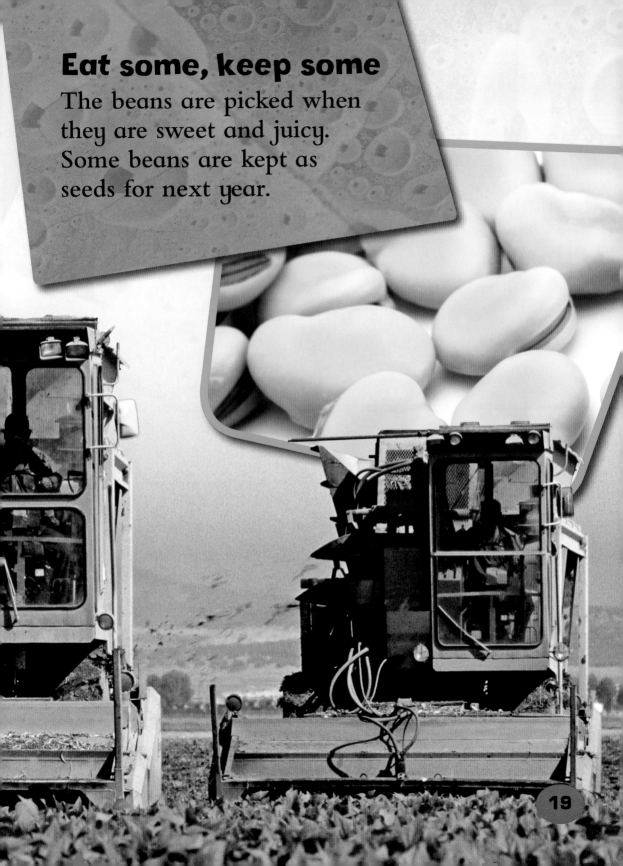

Eat some, keep some

The beans are picked when they are sweet and juicy. Some beans are kept as seeds for next year.

To the Stores

Most beans are sold as food for people to eat. They are taken to a factory, where they are washed and cooked.

How are beans stored?

Some of the beans are put into cans. The rest are frozen and put in plastic bags. The cans and bags are taken in trucks to stores and supermarkets.

 You can buy beans that are still fresh in their pods.

Open up

You have to split open the pod to reach the beans.

Buying beans

You can buy frozen
beans, canned beans,
or beans in jars.

fresh
beans

Glossary

buds Flowers before they open

chemicals Substances that affect things. Chemicals can be used to kill pests such as insects.

insects Small animals with six legs

nectar Sweet juice made by flowers

pod Container that holds seeds while they form

pollen Yellow dust found in the center of flowers

root Part of a plant that takes in water

rots Begins to break up

sap Watery fluid that is found inside plants' stems

seeds Part of the fruit of a plant. A seed can grow into a new plant.

shoot The first two leaves and stem of a plant

stem Part of a plant from which leaves, flowers, and fruit grow

store To keep something, or a place where something is kept

vitamins Tiny parts of food that keep the body healthy

Further Reading

Web Sites

Find out how to grow your own bean plant at:
www.kids-science-experiments.com/watchabean.html

Click on the pictures to see how a plant grows at:
www.zephyrus.co.uk/seed.html

See if you can make a plant grow by playing
this fun game:
www.sciencekids.co.nz/gamesactivities/plantsgrow.html

Books

A Bean's Life by Nancy Dickmann, Heinemann (2010).

The Life Cycle of a Bean by Linda Tagliaferro,
Pebble Books (2007).

The Life Cycle of a Bean by Ruth Thomson,
PowerKids Press (2007).

How a Plant Grows by Bobbie Kalman,
Crabtree Publishing (1997).

Index